C000258926

Cutty Sark Figureheads

The Long John Silver Collection

S. F. Bailey

IAN ALLAN Publishing

Contents

Above:
Cap'n Silver and Mate relaxing on the bridge at The Look-Out.

Cover:
A view of *Cutty Sark's* prow showing the figurehead of Nannie (see page 42). *Photo © Woodmansterne Publications.*

Colour photographs by Brian Morrison
Figurehead drawings by Dave Deamer
Sketches by G. B. Ingham from Sydney Cumbers' unpublished reminiscences

First published 1992

ISBN 0 7110 2111 2

Published by Ian Allan Ltd, Shepperton, Surrey; and printed by Ian Allan Printing Ltd at their works at Coombelands in Runnymede, England.

THE MARITIME TRUST

The Maritime Trust, a registered charity, was established in 1969 to restore, preserve and display historic British ships. The Trust had long acted as managing agent for the clipper ship *Cutty Sark*, and in 1989 the two organisations were merged. The *Cutty Sark* is now the official flagship of the Trust, and the Trust owns another 17 vessels around the country, most of them either on loan or on charter to local organisations, including Captain Scott's *Discovery* now at Dundee.

The Maritime Trust is supported by the Friends of the Maritime Trust. There are reciprocal arrangements with other maritime museums and historic ships which Friends can visit free of charge. Inquiries should be addressed to: The Maritime Trust, 2 Greenwich Church Street, Greenwich, London SE10 9BG (phone: 081 858 2698).

Inquiries about the *Cutty Sark*, which is open throughout the year, should be made to the same address or by phone to 081 853 3589.

AN ICELANDIC FIORD

By the same Author
The Crews of the Cutty Sark

Foreword and Acknowledgements

The clipper ship *Cutty Sark* at Greenwich has on display in its hold a large collection of merchant marine figureheads. It is the largest such collection in Britain, and as far as is known the largest in the world. All of them were collected by one man, Sydney Cumbers, otherwise known as Long John Silver, and he presented them to the *Cutty Sark* in 1953. Although photographs of many of them have appeared as examples in general books about figureheads (for example, *Figureheads* by Giancarlo Costa, published in 1981), there is no book about either the collection as such, or about its collector. This book is an attempt to remedy that defect.

The deed of gift transferring the collection to the *Cutty Sark* is expressed as being between "Sydney Cumbers generally known as 'Captain' Silver and the *Cutty Sark* Preservation Society"; and other than in the biographical chapter 3 references in relation to the collection or the figureheads will be to Cap'n Silver, his own preference and the *nom de mer* by which everyone interested in the subject knew him.

A serious difficulty in dealing with the subject is that whereas naval figureheads are well covered, and naval records about them relatively voluminous, there is very little published about merchant ships, and almost no records about their figureheads. Nearly all the information about the Silver Collection was ferreted out by Cap'n Silver, and in many cases even his persistence failed to unearth anything.

The best and latest book in English, dealing with some merchant marine figureheads as well as naval ones, is *Ships' Figureheads* by Peter Norton, published in 1976. The major English text is *Old Ship Figureheads and Sterns* by L. G. Carr Laughton. This was published in a limited edition in 1925, but a copy of the original edition held in the University of Minnesota Library was reprinted in 1973, and a copy of this is held by the British Library

Cap'n Silver at the front door of The Look-Out, his Gravesend home.

The house at Gravesend was arranged as though it were a ship. These views show (*above*) the hurricane deck with the post-1945 dedication of the collection, (*right*) the foc's'le.

Lending Division. Like almost all books on the subject it is mainly concerned with naval examples, but it does provide overwhelming evidence of the human passion for decorating things. Pauline A. Pinckney published *American Figureheads and Their Carvers* in 1940, and M. V. Brewington published *Ship Carvers of North America* in 1962, and both are acknowledged by Norton as important sources.

This book would not have been possible without the encouragement, support, and very considerable help of Mrs. L. M. Cumbers, the widow of Sydney Cumbers. She not only made available his papers and records but willingly supplemented them with many hours of personal recollections. She played a major part, moreover, in maintaining and cherishing the collection while it was still in their house at Gravesend, and photographs of the interior make clear just how onerous a task that must have been. In many ways this book is a tribute to Mrs. Cumbers as well as to Sydney Cumbers himself.

S. F. Bailey

What are Figureheads?

Silver himself distinguished between carved ornamental stems, which are of great antiquity, and carved detachable figureheads, which seem to have a history of about four hundred years or so. He was an authority on figureheads so defined, but most writers appear to see the detachable figurehead as no more than a technically advanced development of the carved stem, and this book takes the same line.

There seem to have been four strands that have contributed to the practice of mounting figureheads on ships. First, there is the practical matter of how you bring together and fix the materials of which the ship or boat is built. In the case of boats made by hollowing out a big log the problem did not at first arise. When the practice developed of adding to the simple dug-out an extra plank, or strake, along each side to give more depth and allow heavier loading, then it did arise, because the added strakes had to be fixed securely to something at the front and rear. The same result was reached for different reasons in the case of boats made of papyrus reeds on the Nile of ancient Egypt, and still today in places where reed boats are made and used. The reeds have to be bent inwards and upwards and then lashed together at the front and back, forming something like a sort of post. In fact, whatever the type of boat, you finish up with either a vertical or sloping leading edge to the front of the boat. In the case of wooden boats this is almost inevitably a stout piece of timber to which the side timbers are fixed. The

presence on boats of this relatively substantial piece of timber right out front must have been as much a temptation to the decorative instincts of the earliest people as it would be to people today. There is no such structural requirement on land-based vehicles, and although they may be elaborately decorated they do not normally have the equivalent of figureheads, other perhaps than in the form of fancy radiator caps.

Second, there is the human desire to decorate things. The urge to decorate things is perhaps one of the most enduring, and the most endearing, of human traits. Almost every artefact capable of being decorated has been found decorated, no matter how ancient. Combs, buttons, buckles, small pieces of bone or ivory, pieces of wood preserved by chance, pottery, leather, cloth – whatever they are made of, ancient human artefacts, like most modern ones, are almost always found to be decorated in some way. It is one of the commonest facts of archeology. What applies to small personal possessions seems to apply with even more force to large and more important possessions, such as chairs, chariots, houses – and boats.

Third, some things, and for some people most things, are subject to another deep-seated human trait. They are credited with their own special personality. This can range all the way from a fleeting attribute, as when we curse the car for producing an engine failure at midnight on an empty road, to the development of an elaborate persona complete with a name and all the likes and dislikes, fads and fancies, sudden outbursts of jealousy, or of protective love, characteristic of a full human being. Not many inanimate things merit this extreme attribution of personality, but pre-eminent among them are ships, and especially deep-sea ships.

Fourth, it is not easy for people working and living all their lives on land to understand just how unknown, how dangerous, and how dangerously unpredictable the great oceans really are, even today; and how much more unknown, dangerous, and unpredictable they were in the past. Anyone who routinely went to sea had need of all the help and reassurance available, whether natural or supernatural, and from whoever was able to provide it, whether God or devil or merely capricious spirit. Until very recently, and often even now, people reacted to these dangers in the same way. They sought, and still seek, reassurance in a mixture of what is variously described as magic, religion, or superstition but which is in fact an entirely rational attempt to erect guards against the unknowable and to placate the seemingly implacable forces which govern the world. When nothing is known, anything is worth trying.

These strands come together in the attribution of a personality to a ship, in its naming and decoration, and in the development of that decoration into a figurehead. One of the earliest forms of decoration was the use of an *oculus*, or painted eye, on each side of the prow. These occur worldwide, from the earliest times to today. Equally

Right:
The Look-Out included a special room called "Valhalla" which was in practice the main saloon.

6

The foc's'le.

ancient, possibly more so, is the practice of mounting some sort of emblem at the top of the prow timber, called the stem. There is a relief from about 3,000 BC in a tomb at Sakara in Egypt showing a solar disc mounted in this way; there are reliefs from a thousand years later showing a hawk, an ibex, and water birds; and there is an alabaster model of a boat found in the tomb of Tutankhamen of about 1,350 BC which has a carved ibex head as a figurehead. The solar disc, and the ibex, are religious symbols guarding the ship rather than emanations or expressions of the personality of the ship itself, and the same can be true of representations of human beings used as figureheads.

In many cases, of course, the figurehead is in fact consonant with the name of the ship, and there are any number of examples of ships named after wives or daughters with figureheads carved in their likeness. Peter Norton, for instance, has as the frontispiece to his book a charming photograph of John and Anne Gambles standing beneath the bowsprit and figurehead of the three–masted barque *Anne Gambles*, the figurehead being a portrait of Anne Gambles carved by James Brooker of Maryport in Cumberland. The ship was launched in 1862, and the photograph probably taken at about the same time. This was early in the development of photography and John Gambles must have been proud not merely of his ship but of his wife too, and an enterprising character into the bargain to have gone to the trouble of having the picture taken in the first place.

Nevertheless, a figurehead did not necessarily depict the person or character after whom the ship was named. This could be either because the ship had been renamed without the figurehead being changed, or because the figurehead was of some mythical or classical character felt to be appropriate whatever the name of the ship, or because the owner wished to honour someone whose name might (or might not) be connected with the name of the ship. An example of renaming is the *Cutty Sark* herself, whose name was changed to *Ferreira* when she was bought by the Portuguese, and in the Silver collection there is the *Beda*, ex-*Alalura*, ex-*Bertha Marion*.

There are many examples of mythical or classical figures, such as the carving of a winged goddess carrying an oak leaf in the right hand and a laurel leaf in the left which was the figurehead for the Swedish warship *Karl XIII*, or the innumerable lions, rampant or otherwise, which were used for so many seventeenth and eighteenth century ships, or the huge eagle used as a figurehead for the *USS Lancaster* of 1875. A nice variation on this is the *Thermopylae* in the Silver collection, where the figurehead for a ship of that name is simply a Greek warrior.

A good example of a more or less contemporary figure is the figurehead for another US ship, the frigate *Constitution*, which carried a carving of Andrew Jackson, who helped frame the constitution of Tennessee and was President of the US for two terms from 1828. The figureheads in the Silver collection representing Gladstone, Disraeli, or Wilberforce are probably also in this category.

8

Sydney Cumbers the Collector

England has always had its fair share, and sometimes perhaps more than its fair share, of individualists, of people a little larger than life, occasionally people who were a lot larger than life and qualified as eccentrics. The word 'eccentric' does not mean weird or sinister, but merely something which does not revolve symetrically around its centre. A vast range of machinery requires the use of eccentrics, in the form commonly called cams, for its operation and along with the crank the cam is second only to the wheel for doing useful work or keeping things moving. Human eccentrics and individualists perform a similar function in society, and their existence is a mark of a developed society. Pico Iyer (*Time*, 18 January 1988) argued that the eccentric can "be an index of a society's health. The height of British eccentricity, for example, coincided with the height of British power, if only, perhaps, because Britain in its imperial heyday presented so strong a centre from which to depart ... eccentricity is a mark of confidence, accommodated best by a confident society." Certainly Britain in the nineteenth century had a full quota of major eccentrics, but behind them there was on the scene of action a host of straightforward individualists.

One of the outstanding ones spanning the period from late Victorian years to our own day, but now perhaps remembered only by mariners and enthusiasts of nautical history, was Sydney Cumbers, the collector (among other things) of merchant marine figureheads and widely, indeed internationally, known as Long John Silver. Sydney Cumbers was born at the family home in London on 7 October 1875, the third son and fifth child of Charles and Matilda Cumbers. There were seven children in all, four boys and three girls. He died, the last surviving son of the family, in 1959, and over that long period saw many changes and accomplished much in his own right.

The Cumbers family was a reasonably comfortable middle–class family, and Charles Cumbers was the founder and senior partner in the firm of Johnstone and Cumbers, printing ink manufacturers, which he founded in 1863. He was a good and enterprising businessman, and from a small start the firm expanded steadily until it became relatively large and well known in the trade. Sydney joined the firm after he left school in 1893 and apparently showed considerable aptitude. In 1921 the firm was reorganised as a private limited company, with Sydney, then 46, as Chairman and Managing Director. The factory premises were at Sugar House Lane, in Stratford, London E15. In March 1941 they were totally destroyed in an air raid, but the firm recovered in temporary premises, and in 1944 bought the nearby premises of Blackwell and Company, manufacturers of screen inks and poster paints. Later Blackwell and Company became a wholly owned subsidiary of

Sydney's father, Charles Cumbers.

9

Right:
Sydney Cumbers as a boy.

Johnstone and Cumbers. The official journal of the Society of British Printing Ink Manufacturers, in issues recording the death of Sydney Cumbers (November 1959), the 100th anniversary of the firm (November 1963), and its 112th anniversary (August 1975), made it clear that Sydney Cumbers was a widely respected, astute, and much loved businessman, although the 1959 obituary in particular gave full treatment of his activities as Long John Silver as well. They could hardly do otherwise, but the fact remained that for much of the year he was an able and energetic businessman in London, and for the remainder was the dashing, flamboyant Cap'n Silver at Gravesend.

To finish off the story of Johnstone and Cumbers, the firm continued under that name until August 1980, when it changed to J & C Printing Inks. It was two or three years later joined with Richardson Printing Inks, although the two companies continued with their separate names. They were later briefly taken over by Dufay Reprographics, which in turn was acquired by A. R. Gibbon. The firm now operates as part of the Gibbon

The three Cumbers brothers who joined the family firm — Frederick, the eldest, then Ernest, then Sydney, the third youngest.

group under the name Gibbon JCR Inks and Coatings Limited at Kempston, Bedford.

When Sydney was born the family lived at 31 Buckingham Road in Hackney, but by the time of his earliest recorded recollections they had moved to Croydon; and by the time he was six they had also taken a house at Westbrook, then a small village near Margate. In his own words: "From December to June we only 'existed' at Croydon and July to December we 'lived' at Westbrook". As he gives an account of at least one Christmas spent at Westbrook it really does seems to have been six months at Croydon and six months at Westbrook. Soon after they were established at Westbrook the seven Cumbers children linked up there with an even larger family, the Bridges. They had thirteen children, ten boys and three girls, although when they first met the two youngest boys, twins, and the three girls had not been born. What eventually became a group – gang is not perhaps the right word – of twenty children seems to have mixed together very well and must have provided an admirable environment for a boy who was later to describe himself as being of a "nervous, temperamental nature". As a matter of interest one of the Bridges twins subsequently became Sir Ernest Bridges, a Captain in the RM Line and Commodore of Convoys in the 1939–45 War.

It is quite clear that the annual six months at Westbrook served to fix Sydney Cumbers' attention on ships and the sea. In the circumstances it would probably have happened to most children, and like many children he began to acquire model ships and collect things at about the age of eight. What made him different was that he went on doing it for the rest of his life and, moreover, kept his childhood models through to the end. His third model, a single-cylinder working steamer 3ft 6in long, fired by methylated spirit, and eventually named *Sidonian*, marked a significant change in his life.

Because of his disposition he was not sent to school until he was ten, prior to that being educated at home by his eldest sister Louise. Then he went to a small preparatory school nearby. At the Christmas after his first year there he and his youngest brother, Percy, were each given a toy gun. These had a spring for ejecting whatever you cared to put in the barrel and, for greater realism, there was a percussion cap simultaneously operated by the trigger. While conducting a "pheasant" shoot in their garden Sydney suddenly found that he could not see properly with his left eye. The local chemist recommended seeing their family doctor, the doctor recommended seeing an eye specialist, and several specialists were seen. The conclusion reached was that a fragment from the percussion cap had entered his eye, and that the eye would have to be removed.

His father allowed Sydney to choose which specialist he would like to undertake the operation, and also decided it should take place at home – this was in 1887, when such matters were a lot less regulated than they are today. The operation took place literally on the kitchen table, and there were no complications. The piece of the percussion cap was duly found in the eyeball, and that was that. Sydney had one usable eye, and one glass one.

To help overcome the shock and discouragement which this loss might have produced Sydney was encouraged to make more of his interest in shipping and in models, and it was to help this process along that his father gave him the working model steamer *Sidonian*. Because with only one eye he could no longer judge distances and was therefore no good at ball games, he used his spare time spotting ships and checking their movements from Lloyds List. By his early 'teens he was the acknowledged expert at the centre of a group at school, which included the geography master, studying the details of pretty well everything connected with shipping. He left his first preparatory school for a larger one, also at Margate, then went to another at Croydon, then finished at Kings College School in London. At all of these he was a day boy, with none of the stresses or loss of family support entailed by being a boarder, and at all of them he maintained and strengthened his passion for everything to do with the sea and the merchant marine – he objected to calling it the merchant navy. By 1893, when he left school

The Look-Out — Cap'n Silver at the wheel.

by small grasshoppers which we caught in butter-
fly nets at the scene of action), the next thing
to consider was our provender.

This would consist of enough sandwiches,
bacon and eggs, cakes, etc., to feed an army corps,
as it must be borne in mind that we were all
youngsters and had very sturdy appetites.   Apart
from the food, we had to transport tablecloths,
cups, saucers, knives, forks, saucepans and the
inevitable frying pan.

So by the time we set forth to catch the
8.14 from Margate Station to Birchington, we
resembled African native carriers.

Here we added to our burdens by purchasing
from the local shop ginger beer, lemonade,
literally by the dozen, and then began the final
foot slogging to the scene of the encampment,
some three miles away.   By the time it was
reached we were quite ready to start on breaking
a bottle of lemonade and, having quenched our
thirst, we proceeded to mark out our encampment,
making a sort of stockade with large bulrushes

Extract from Sydney Cumbers' reminiscences — going on a picnic.

12

Bathing Women.

We must not forget the cry of the

Bathing Women who were in charge of the Ladies'

Bathing Machine, which went like this:

"Come to your Martha,
          Come - come - come,
The water's so warm in the
          sun - sun - sun,
Don't shiver, my dear,
          There's nothing to fear,
So come to your Martha,
          Catch hold of the rope."

Martha was usually a very strong, hefty

creature, who grabbed her victim as she came

timidly down the steps under the canopy behind

the machine and with one swoop ducked her

under the water.

"MARTHA"

Extract from Sydney Cumbers' reminiscences — bathing machines.

The conclusion was that a part of the percussion cap, which had "burst", had made a clean bull's-eye of the pupil of my eye !

The unanimous verdict — the eye would have to be "removed".

So that was that.

My Father asked me which of the specialists I liked the most, so I chose a Mr Vernon, a kindly middle-aged man.

Then to ease my feelings, he arranged for the operation to be performed at home, which meant, of course, domestic upheaval.

Arrangements were made with our M.O. and on the appointed day, down came Mr Vernon ....

I remember when he surveyed the "temporary ward" he thought the table would not be large enough, and after looking at others, finally decided on the kitchen table, much to Jane Hawkins' (our old cook) surprise ! She wasn't quite sure if it was quite the right thing for such an important event.

So on the table I went. As was the custom

Extract from Sydney Cumbers' reminiscences — preparing for the eye operation

then the anaesthetist put a plug of wool
soaked in chloroform over my face, told me
to breathe in through my nose and in due
time, I was "off" ! -

The operation was a complete success
and the offending piece of the cap discovered
well and truly embedded in the eye.

It was quite over a month before I could
get out and about again, and some six months
before I tried a glass eye.

Having missed more than half that term at
school, it was decided it wasn't worth while
going for the remainder, so I had a grand long
holiday which compensated somewhat !

The reaction or "backwash" to anything of
this kind didn't, at first, manifest itself.

From the moment it happened I found myself
a sort of "family hero" - fussed over and
receiving all the attention - friends calling in
and making enquiries - in fact, the centre of
attraction.

But as time went on I began to find I

Extract from Sydney Cumbers' reminiscences — after the eye operation.

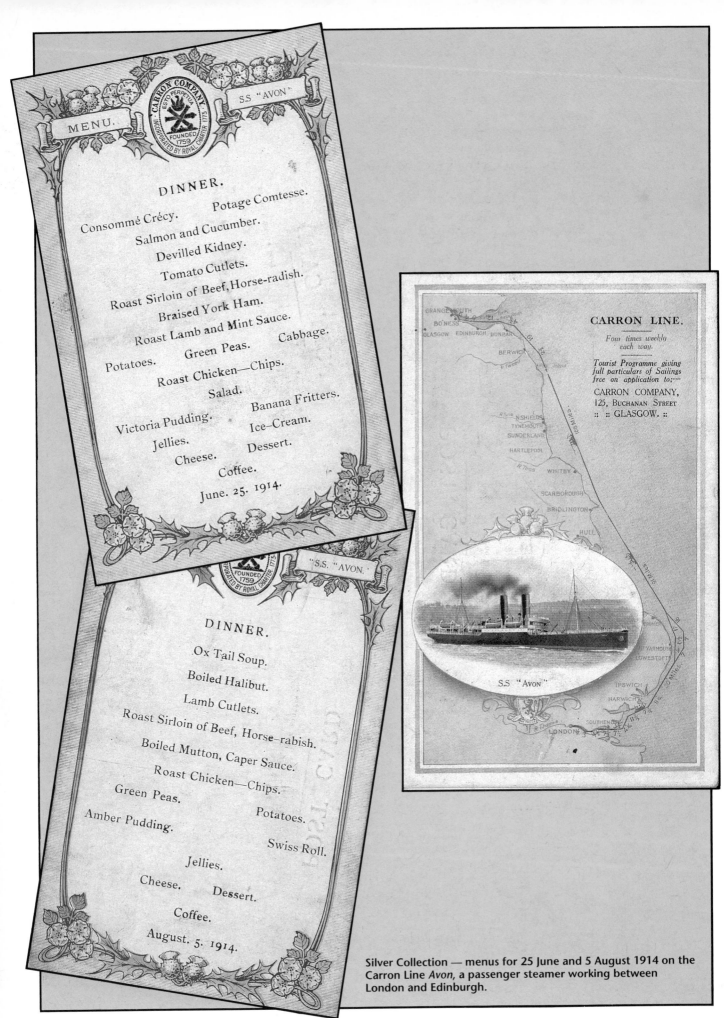

MENU.

CARRON COMPANY
ESTO PERPETUA
INCORPORATED BY ROYAL CHARTER 1773
FOUNDED 1759.

S.S. "AVON."

DINNER.

Consommé Crécy.   Potage Comtesse.

Salmon and Cucumber.

Devilled Kidney.

Tomato Cutlets.

Roast Sirloin of Beef, Horse-radish.

Braised York Ham.

Roast Lamb and Mint Sauce.

Potatoes.   Green Peas.   Cabbage.

Roast Chicken—Chips.

Salad.

Victoria Pudding.   Banana Fritters.

Ice-Cream.

Jellies.   Dessert.

Cheese.

Coffee.

June. 25. 1914.

FOUNDED 1759.
INCORPORATED BY ROYAL CHARTER 1773.

"S.S. "AVON."

DINNER.

Ox Tail Soup.

Boiled Halibut.

Lamb Cutlets.

Roast Sirloin of Beef, Horse-rabish.

Boiled Mutton, Caper Sauce.

Roast Chicken—Chips.

Green Peas.

Potatoes.

Amber Pudding.

Swiss Roll.

Jellies.

Cheese.   Dessert.

Coffee.

August. 5. 1914.

CARRON LINE.

*Four times weekly
each way.*

*Tourist Programme giving
full particulars of Sailings
free on application to:—*

CARRON COMPANY,
125, BUCHANAN STREET
:: :: GLASGOW. ::

S.S. "AVON"

Silver Collection — menus for 25 June and 5 August 1914 on the
Carron Line *Avon*, a passenger steamer working between
London and Edinburgh.

to join the family firm, he was well under way as a serious collector.

In essence he was simply a collector but one who was even more than most collectors untroubled by worries about the immediate practicalities of housing what he collected. When figureheads came his way, he added them to the collection. Two of the figureheads in his collection he had in fact seen as a boy of about seven or eight. These were the Duchess, and Lord Beaconsfield, which were kept under the eaves of the sail loft of Beeching and Moses, the shipbuilders at Ramsgate; but he only acquired them many years later after Ramsgate Council had taken over the Beeching and Moses yard, which formed part of Ramsgate harbour. His own pertinacity led him to many, but once he began to be known friends, acquaintances, or even total strangers, would get in touch and let him know where one might be found. Nevertheless he was initially, and to the end, primarily a collector of merchant marine relics, mementos, and curios. The figureheads just happened to be much larger, more colourful and, when assembled in any quantity, more overwhelming than the rest of the collection.

After he left school and went to work, he was encouraged by his sister Louise, whom he described as musically most gifted, to study in his spare time singing and elocution at the Guildhall School of Music. He also after a while stopped taking his holidays with the family at Westbrook and began to launch out on his own.

His first major trip was in 1898, when he was coming up to 23, and it was, inevitably, a trip by steamer to Gibraltar, the Canary Islands, the Moroccan coast and Tangier, and other ports of call. He enjoyed it enormously, and during it became friendly with Aleck Berens, a professional artist who was on his honeymoon, and characteristically retained the friendship for the rest of their lives. Berens much later wrote an account of it and of one particular incident which gives some idea of what Sydney was like as a young man. They were in a desert village outside the local inn, about four hours riding from Mogador, surrounded by a mixture of camel drivers, miscellaneous travellers and loafers when Sydney, whom Berens called "The Boy", came out of the inn and started chaffing and larking with people in the crowd. He was apparently well known, and well appreciated, for this. After some exchanges with one exceptionally tall camel driver Sydney suddenly shouted that the man had stolen his eye, standing with arms stretched out so that everyone could see he had only one eye. This naturally led to a lot of disturbance and excited arguments which Sydney quelled by calling out that he could see his eye in the man's turban. He hustled him into the centre of the crowd, searched the turban and then clapped his hands to his face and slowly removed them so that everyone could see he now had two eyes. It was a well enough executed piece of sleight of hand to deceive many of the crowd, including the camel driver. Sydney could perhaps have got the idea for this trick from Rider Haggard's *King Solomon's Mines*, published about twelve years earlier, in which Captain Goode baffles some tribesmen by removing and replacing

Model made by Sydney Cumbers, aged 10, after he lost his eye. Made of a piece of firewood and his sister's hatpins and hair.

Silver Collection — model of a galleon made of leather.

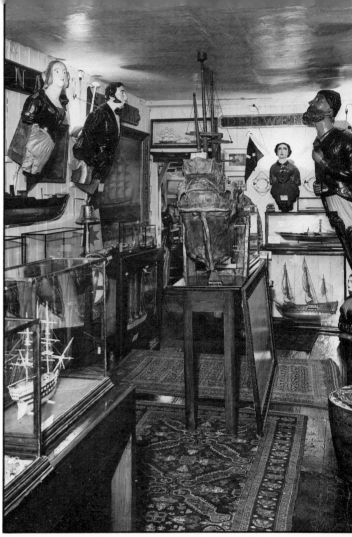

Right:
The Foc's'le, leather model of galleon at centre.

his false teeth in a similar way but all the evidence is that young Sydney Cumbers had more than enough high spirits to think of things like this for himself.

Somewhat after this Moroccan trip he organised a room where he was living in London as a Moroccan room, with the ceiling painted to simulate a North African sky and elaborately furnished with Moroccan artefacts. They were all genuine and he always claimed he had bought all of them in London, mostly in street markets.

Although he made many further trips, all by sea, the only ones of which he left any written account was one to Russia in 1901, and one probably about a couple of years later, when he went to Iceland. The trip to Russia took him by sea up the Baltic to St. Petersburg, where he stayed for a while, then by train to Moscow. As always, he seems to have made friends along the way, including Baron Knoop, head of the large cotton firm Thoedore Knoop and Sons, from whom he borrowed £5 in order to get back to London.

The Iceland holiday was something of a challenge in that he had to learn to ride a horse because at the time it was the only means of transport in that country. He took his riding lessons at St. John's Wood Barracks with a

The Look-Out — a view of the bridge.

battery of the Royal Horse Artillery and eventually became good enough to be included, surreptitiously and improperly, in a formal review of the Battery on Wormwood Scrubs.

On 26 August 1905 he married Ada Mary Madders. He was then 29 and she was 27. The marriage was not successful and they separated. He later met, and on 16 March 1937 married, Louisa (usually called Lois) May Mallett, who remained his inseparable companion until his death in 1959.

Although the outstanding feature of the Silver Collection was the group of figureheads, the fact is that it would have been an extraordinary enough collection even without them, and its setting still more extraordinary. A total of 101 figureheads, some of them huge, over a hundred models of ships, including nine of the paddle-steamer pleasure boats operating between London and Southend, Ramsgate, and Margate, name boards, ships wheels, lights, lead lines and log lines, lifebuoys, pictures, documents, compasses, bells, miniature telegraphs,

The Boy & The Pariahs

Above:
Sketch by Aleck Berens of young Sydney Cumbers "finding" his glass eye in the camel driver's turban, Morocco, 1898.

Left:
Sydney Cumbers in Morocco, 1898 from a sketch by Aleck Berens

Top and centre right:
The *Sunday Graphic,* 8 December 1935, reporting the opening of
The Look-Out for visitors.

Bottom right:
The *Kent Messenger,* 14 December 1935, reporting the opening
of The Look-Out.

The Thames steamer *Primrose* which Sydney Cumbers took
down river to pick up the boat to Russia in 1901.

Cap'n Silver and Mate at the entrance to The Look-Out.

shark's teeth, harpoons, paintings, glass rolling pins given
by sailors as keepsakes, flags, telescopes, a sextant,
chronometers – everything was there, including a stuffed
rat and a pickled cockroach to lend versimilitude; and all
this was well displayed in a small house on the riverside
at Gravesend. In all there were over a thousand items.
There are several accounts of what it was like, and many
photographs of it have survived.

The collection was housed at The Look-Out at
Gravesend. This was a house which was part of the
Clarendon Hotel on the river front, and he took it on a 21
year lease in 1932. The building was semi-derelict and a
lot of work was needed before it was fit for his purpose;
and then, of course, he had to move the collection in and
arrange it to his exacting taste. He finally opened it to
friends and acquaintances, of whom he had a great many,
on Saturday 7 December 1935. It was arranged, and the
interior named, as though it were a ship, with a foc's'le,
half deck, well deck, quarter deck, and bridge, with one
special room called "Valhalla" which was in practice the
main saloon. In 1948 he added an area named the 'tween
deck. And everywhere, on walls, on floors, on shelves, on
plinths, hanging from the ceiling, everywhere where there
was space, was his collection, dominated by the
figureheads because of their number and size. It really was
an extraordinary collection, in an extraordinary setting.

SHIP THAT WILL NEVER SAIL

The story of the ship that will never go to sea, told on the opposite page, is illustrated in these pictures. It was "launched" yesterday in a backyard at Gravesend by Captain Silver, seen (left) with Lady Muskerry, widow of the famous sailor-peer, and Mrs. Silver. Left: Some of the guests.

Chief Officer A. F. Jackson (H.M.S. Worcester) and Captain W. M. Corbett give a toast at the "launching" of the new ship.

...ated by Dr. P. Mellowes, with Lady ...y's "launching" of the Gravesend ...in Silver, the "skipper," formerly ...n a merchant steamer.

SUNDAY GRAPHIC
December 8, 1935.

CAPTAIN SILVER— HIS SHIP

It is the Most Luxurious Liner That Will Never Go to Sea

THERE is one man who was so fond of the sea and things nautical that he has made his home into the replica of an ocean-going liner—and the most luxurious liner that will never go to sea.

He is Captain Silver, of Gravesend, a London company director, who formerly served on a merchant steamer. Yesterday one of the most remarkable private collections of ship models and nautical souvenirs ever seen in Great Britain was opened to a few friends.

Opposite the little harbour where Gravesend shrimp boats are moored a disused house and what was a derelict back yard three weeks ago now looks like a liner.

Entrance is made through a gangway, on either si... ...e crew's quarters, the fo'c'stle and the poop.

The main saloon is called the Val Halla—a hall in which is shown a rare collection of figureheads of famous windjammers and woodenwalls.

Fish at the Portholes

The bridge has a companion-way at the entrance and forms the upstairs part of the house. Working steering equipment is the same as in a steamship and there is a full-sized funnel as a background.

Live fish in specially-made tanks swim by portholes, and models of ships, also seen through the portholes, give the impression that one is at sea. Telegraphs and compasses are all in working order, and the bridge looks out on to the river Thames.

Aboard the Look Out, as this "ship" is called, there are winter gardens and chart house.

The "crew" of six, including a bosun and deck boy, act chiefly as stewards to the visitors. Trinity House pilots who "went aboard" yesterday were amazed at the careful attention which has been paid to detail.

Orders to the Crew

Captain Silver, who wears a black eye-shade and a tiepin consisting of skull and crossbones, has only one eye and is therefore unable to pursue his love for the sea except in this way. He stands on the bridge, look-ing towards the Thames, and bellows orders

---

The Strangest Ship That Never Sailed The Sea

"LONG JOHN" SILVER IN COMMAND

OLD HOUSE FITTED OUT LIKE LINER

SOME Gravesend pilots looked through a port hole and saw a picture of undersea life with fish gliding through weeds around what appeared to be the yards of a wrecked sailing ship.

This incident occurred on Saturday and it was the finishing touch to a per-fect illusion. For these pilots were not in a ship at sea. They were in an old house near the famous Royal Terrace Pier, Gravesend.

Some time ago Mr. Sydney Silver, a Lon-don business man, bought it and, at great expense, fitted it out like a ship, so that he could spend his week-ends in an atmosphere of the sea. He calls it the s.s. Look Out, and the bridge is so arranged that it over-looks Bawley Bay and the Thames. It is a perfect replica of an ocean-going liner and the fittings of real ships—wheel, telegraphs, lights, binnacle, etc.—lend the correct nau-tical touch

Through the portholes live fish can be seen, swimming among the weeds and around the "yards" of "wrecked" sailing ships.

The fish and the "wrecks" are in specially arranged tanks.

On each side of the bridge are two scale models of 28ft. life boats, which help to set off the realistic teak decks below.

Abaft the wheel is a large funnel, com-plete with gleaming syren ...

The river ...

CAPTAIN SILVER

Water colours by Aleck Berens of Cap'n Silver for the "launching" of The Look-Out, 1936.

The Look-Out — looking through to the quarter deck. The arch is the jawbone of a Greenland right whale.

Above left:
The Look-Out — part of the hurricane deck, showing whaling harpoons.

SIDONIAN

The Look-Out — another corner of the hurricane deck.

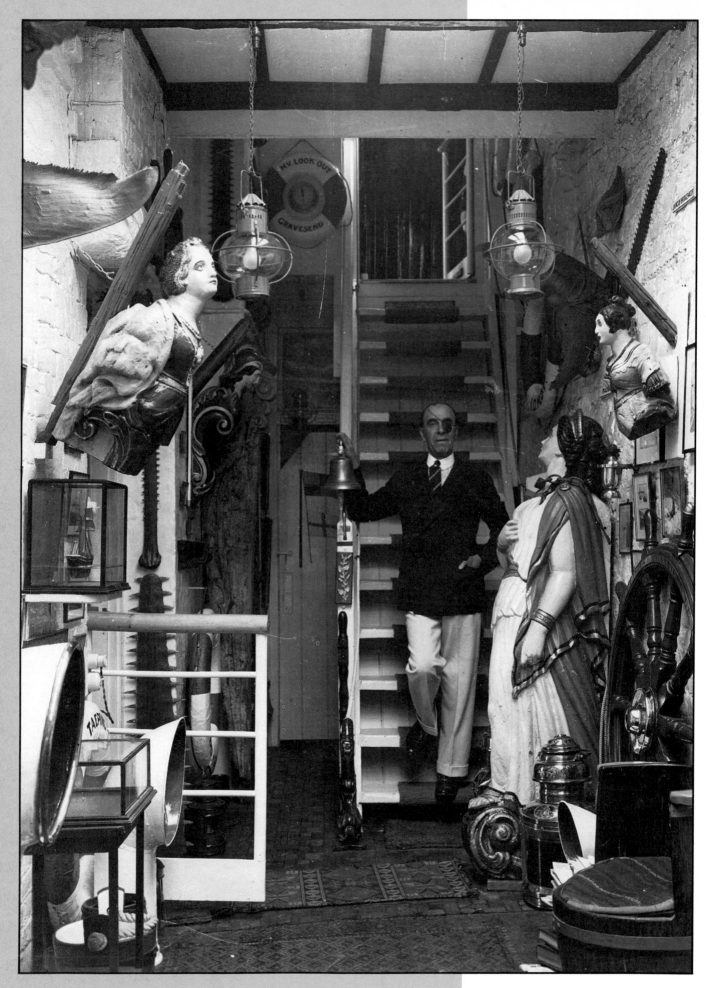

Cap'n Silver coming down the companion way from the bridge.

Dominating even the figureheads was the redoubtable figure of Sydney Cumbers or Long John Silver — Cap'n Silver — himself. He was a well-built, lean man with a strong face accentuated by a black eye patch. At some point during the 1914-1918 War, after a bad bout of eye inflamation, he discarded the glass eye because, he said: "One becomes quite accustomed to seeing the wounded going around minus arms, legs, and eyes, so I did not feel quite so conspicuous when I sometimes wore a black patch". He continues his account of throwing away the glass eye: "The psychological effect of this was most extraordinary. Once I had made up my mind to leave it out, I became Master of myself – all my previous nervous mannerisms and self-consciousness seemed to melt away ... Of course, I received several nicknames – such as 'Captain Cook' and 'Nelson', but 'Long John Silver' seemed to be the favourite amongst my friends, so I adopted it as my 'nom-de-mer' – and this is roughly the story of how Long John Silver came into being."

Bearing in mind the boyish joker of fifteen or so years earlier described by Aleck Berens, the new man must have been quite outstanding. Moreover he added to the effect by wearing, in his Long John Silver role, a tie–pin with skull and crossbones, smoking cigarettes through an amber holder, frequently singing sea shanties in a strong baritone, and calling masterfully for grog when the time was ripe. He also, later, had a mast on a small plot across the road by the river's edge from which he flew signals of varying degrees of facetiousness, although the standard

The Look-Out — Cap'n Silver on the bridge.

Cap'n Silver (left) on the bridge chatting with Captain Alex Horsley, a Trinity House Pilot. The middle notice on the right reads: "Anyone caught putting ash or cigarette ends down any ventilator will be thrown overboard".

25

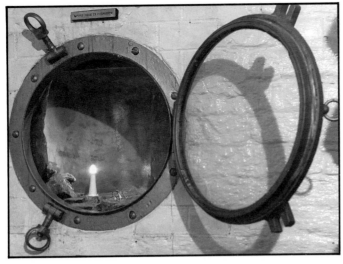

A port hole on The Look-Out. Some were kept closed with fish tanks behind to give the illusion of being under water. One open one had a small crocodile peering out.

Right:
Cap'n Silver, the *Golden Cherubs,* and painting of John Jacobs, the original owner of the ship.

The Look-Out — Cap'n Silver with model of ship.

one was "Welcome, come on board". In the best sense it was a complete and lovingly detailed theatrical presentation, and he maintained it meticulously.

In particular, he maintained the name Long John Silver, and in a mass of correspondence about the collection every letter is addressed to Captain Silver, or sometimes just Long John Silver. There is even one, on 4 September 1947, from the London office of Time-Life International, which was doing a story with pictures about him, which was addressed to: "Capt. L. J. Silver, The Look-Out, Gravesend"; and after thanking him for his help the writer went on to ask,in all innocence, what the initials L. J. stood for. Similarly a letter from Sir Gerald Barry, the Director General of the Festival of Britain, was addressed to Captain L. John Silver on 3 August 1951. Barry may, of course, have simply known of and respected the curious split between Sydney Cumbers, businessman of London, and Long John Silver, collector of marine memorabilia of Gravesend. On the other hand, many people who knew of him in the one role did not know of him in the other. In any case, as far as can be seen, whenever he wrote or spoke in connection with his collection it was always in the Long John Silver role.

In the many accounts of what a visit to The Look-Out was like, some of them staid in the manner of occasional writings fifty and sixty years ago, the sheer exuberance of Cap'n Silver shines through every time. Something of his personality can be illustrated by an incident from just before 1939. He was on his way home in London from a business meeting, and called in at a shop to collect a long

Silver Collection — model of the tug *Anglia*, nicknamed "Three Finger Jack". In 1878 it towed the barge with Cleopatra's Needle from the Bay of Biscay, where it had been nearly lost in a storm, back to London.

handled net to use in his aquarium. As he came out of the shop some small boys cheekily asked if he was going fishing. Without hesitation he said he was, and would they like to come along. They thought they would; and for the next hour or so a party consisting of several grubby boys and one soberly dressed middle-aged city gentleman fished for sticklebacks in Kensington Round Pond. He was not merely slightly larger than life, he relished it as well and had no hesitation in showing that relish. He was, as many people said and as his widow so many years later still reiterates, fun to have around. And he had an unrivalled and encyclopaedic knowledge of ships and shipping, with an endless fund of stories and anecdotes to go with it.

In September 1952 he was told the lease of The Look-Out would expire the following year, and could not be renewed. By then he was 77, and however youthful his spirits might be no one is immortal. The problem was not so much finding another base in Gravesend for himself and his wife, but finding a secure and permanent home for what was now an internationally known collection. There were collectors in the USA who would have liked to take it over, but he wanted to keep the collection in England and, if possible, closely associated with the Thames. The Borough of Gravesend might have provided a home, but it

was not quite what he wanted. The opportunity he was looking for came with the formation in 1952 of the Cutty Sark Society, established to take over the old clipper ship, renovate her and put her on display to the public at Greenwich. This, he thought, would provide a proper home for the collection; and the newly formed Society was willing to accept this unexpected responsibility.

The timing was, however, a little awkward. Although a committee had been formed in 1951 to raise money to build a permanent dry dock at Greenwich where the *Cutty Sark* could be restored and exhibited to the public, the formal transfer of the ship to the Cutty Sark Society took place only in May 1953, and a dry dock could not be begun until early 1954. This meant that the Silver Collection, although assured of a permanent home in due course, would have to be stored somewhere until the *Cutty Sark* was not merely safely docked but ready to receive it.

The collection was formally handed over to the Society on 29 July 1953 at Thames House adjoining The Look-Out, into which Mr. and Mrs. Cumbers were to move. It was a relatively elaborate ceremony, as befitted the occasion, with a marquee on Thames House lawn and the Chairman of the Cutty Sark Society, Henry Barraclough, the chairman of its maintenance committee, General Sir Frederick Browning, the Trustees of the Society, and others, present. The deed of gift was handed over and for the tea party which followed there was an iced cake two-and-a-half feet long in the form of the *Cutty Sark* herself.

Silver Collection — life-line from a *Titanic* lifeboat.

Silver Collection Visitor's Book – entry by Beryl Madeline Read, a descendent of the American Indian Princess Pocohontas, who died at Gravesend in March 1617.

10th June '1??

I came to Gravesend to visit the burial place of my ancestor, Princess Pocohontas. Fate led me to "The Look Out" where among Captain Silver's unusual collection was a ships figure-head of Hiawatha another Red Indian.

This has been for me a most delightful afternoon. which I am sure I will always remember, and I hope to take advantage of Mrs Silver's very kind invitation to return.

Beryl Madeline Read.

This, a nice touch, was "launched" by Lady Bridges, the widow of Commodore Sir Ernest Bridges, his boyhood friend, and the formal cake cutting was done by Sir Frederick Browning using one of the collection items, a sword made from the boney beak of a swordfish. After the tea, at which local shrimps were served, there were sea songs led by Cap'n Silver, and there was a last visit to the collection in The Look-Out. And that was it. A strange and highly idiosyncratic episode in the history of the Thames had after nearly a quarter of a century come gracefully to an appropriate end.

Soon afterwards the collection was packed and stored, partly in the National Maritime Museum, until 1957 when the *Cutty Sark* was opened to the public. Most of the figureheads, which had where necessary been cleaned up and repainted, and a selection of pieces from the collection, were then exhibited on board. The number of figureheads on display has slowly been increased as restoration and repainting has continued, and the models and other pieces on display are varied from time to time. The remainder of the collection is kept by the Maritime Trust (which now owns the *Cutty Sark*) in its store.

The Cumbers' move into Thames House was completed in 1954, with the top floor organised as Silver's room, complete with personal treasures withheld from the collection transferred to the *Cutty Sark*, such as the old *Sidonian* model ship given him by his father, his telescope and binoculars, and personal pictures, photographs, and scrap books. Soon after the move he suffered a serious stroke which affected him badly physically, although not mentally. He died on 10 September 1959, less than a month before his 84th birthday.

View of the river from a port-hole of The Look-Out, drawn by G. B. Ingham and used for The Look-Out letter heading.

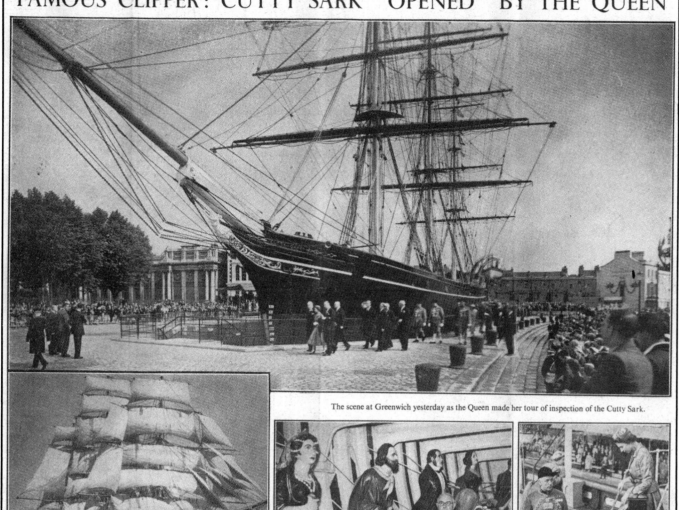

18 ★★★ 8 THE TIMES WEDNESDAY JUNE 26 1957

FAMOUS CLIPPER: CUTTY SARK "OPENED" BY THE QUEEN

The scene at Greenwich yesterday as the Queen made her tour of inspection of the Cutty Sark.

Above:
The Queen inspecting the Silver Collection on 25 June 1957.
The Times

Christmas card for 1953, after the Silver Collection was transferred to the *Cutty Sark*. Drawn by G. B. Ingham. The message reads: "With a full cargo of good wishes for Christmas and the New Year from Cap'n Silver and the Mate".

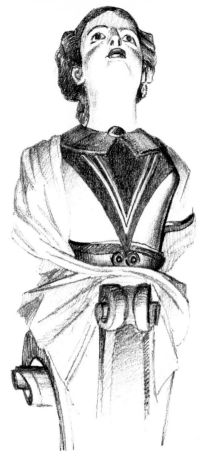

Restoring Figureheads

The present day carver who restored and repaired much of the Long John Silver Collection for exhibition on the *Cutty Sark* is J. F. (Jack) Whitehead, of Wootton Creek in the Isle of Wight. He was born in 1913 and is still very active and busy. The photograph shows him at work in July 1990 on a new carving of Charles Darwin. He took up the work as a full-time professional relatively late in life. He had, he says, always amused himself by doing wood carving, and during the 1939-45 war while he was at Minchinhampton near Stroud received about a couple of months tuition from Adrian Alinson, a fairly well–known painter and sculptor. A little before this his right hand had been injured by an aeroplane propellor during his service with the RAF, and the surgeon recommended that he kept up his wood carving as a form of physiotherapy. After the war he joined the film industry, doing special effects and keeping his wood carving as a spare-time hobby. By then he had his home at Wootton Creek, and a friend who had built himself a boat asked Whitehead if he thought he could carve a figurehead for it. Jack could not see why a figurehead should be all that different from any other carving, and agreed to try. He made this, his very first figurehead, a mermaid, and it was successful. The owner of the boat and his wife were proposing to sail her to New Zealand, the local photographers and press took an interest and, more to the point, took photographs of the boat and its new figurehead which were published in *Yachts and*

Yachting. From that publication alone he received over twenty requests from people all over Britain who wanted a figurehead but had not known they are still being carved.

He kept on with the film work for a while, but slowly began to realise he had more orders for carving than he could possibly manage in his spare time. Without too much of a struggle he threw over the film work and went full time as a carver, and has stayed that way ever since. His connection with the *Cutty Sark* began in 1969 when Frank G. G. Carr, who had three years earlier retired as Director of the National Maritime Museum asked him if he thought he could restore the battered and dismembered figure of "Nannie", from the *Cutty Sark* itself, which had been discovered stowed away on the ship. He did this very well, as anyone can see who inspects her on board in the 'tween deck near the entrance, and as a result was asked to try his hand at other damaged items in the Silver Collection. Some of these had deteriorated while in store at the National Maritime Museum because the wood used for figureheads is normally a softwood, being easier to carve, and also lighter. The latter is important, especially if the figurehead is more or less life sized and if made of hardwood could weigh up to half a ton or more. This, mounted well out in front, could seriously unbalance a small ship. Softwoods do, however, easily and rapidly deteriorate if kept in anything less than ideal conditions.

Repairing and restoring a figurehead poses several problems. First, there is the question of what it looked like originally. There may be photographs or drawings of it which will settle the matter; but there may not be, and in these cases, which are the majority, the carver has to do the best he can from studying the lines of what has been left. If all else fails, he uses his imagination.

A figurehead of Charles Darwin being carved by Jack Whitehead, July 1990.

Far left , top: Jack Whitehead starting work on a restoration.

Far left , bottom: Jack Whitehead in a corner of his workshop.

Left and below: A figurehead prepared for restoration, showing blocks of wood glued to back and side.

Second, there is the problem of getting the replacement pieces to fit in smoothly so that, if possible, the repair cannot be detected. The usual method is to clean and prepare the area of the original carving which is to be extended by new work, and then glue into position a relatively large piece of new wood. Once this is safely married to the old wood, it can be carved into the desired shape. If there is a detectable line between the old and the new, it will be covered by paint before the repaired figurehead is exhibited to the public.

Third, this process of repair and restoration raises some very delicate questions about authenticity. Until recently a badly damaged antique was seen as an antique in need of repair, and not as an antique which should be preserved in its damaged state. It is not, unfortunately, easy to define the point at which, either aesthetically or as a matter of historical record, restoration becomes unacceptable. Very slight damage can perhaps be left unrepaired, especially if there is a story to the damage and if it is so slight as not to affect the overall impression of the object concerned. A sculpture where the main interest lies in the carving of the torso and its muscles, but where in the passage of time the head or arms have been lost, can perhaps be left like that; and the *Venus de Milo* has been so left. On the other hand the *Discus Thrower*, where the head is arguably less important than *Venus*'s arms, has had an alien head grafted on to it, and looking in the wrong direction at that. Possibly a more careful and more anatomically correct restoration of the *Discus Thrower*'s head would be less jarring, but the problem of whether to restore or not remains.

Long John Silver seems to have taken the practical line that if the damage was not too great, and if he could be personally confident that the restoration maintained the original intentions, he would restore; and the *Cutty Sark* has inherited with the collection the same line of practicality. The question is not, however, an academic one. At least one dealer in figureheads approached Jack Whitehead some years ago asking him to "knock out" some figureheads leaving them unpainted so that his own expert could "distress" them (his words in both cases) and export them to America as genuine. Jack refused the offer, but there were no doubt other less fussy carvers willing to take it up. Certainly Cap'n Silver refers occasionally to refusing offers of figureheads which he rejected as fakes, and there is little to suggest that the passage of fifty or sixty years has made dealers more scrupulous.

Figureheads during their working lives were repainted regularly, normally as a voyage neared its end. A ship with twenty or thirty years of service could therefore have as many layers of paint on its figurehead, and Whitehead says twenty or more layers of paint is not uncommon. The task of achieving the right colours in the restored figurehead is the relatively straightforward but tedious one of removing paint layer by layer until the bottom one is reached. It is clear from Carr Laughton that the old sailing ships in their prime, and especially the larger or more important ones, were highly colourful and the very important ones would carry gold leaf as well as mere paint. In most cases a reasonably accurate idea of the original colours can be obtained, and the restored figurehead repainted accordingly.

32

Notes on the Colour Plates

These notes are based on Silver's records, supplemented in some cases by later information. Some of them are very sparse, for the good reason that even Silver was unable to find out much about them; and there are a further forty–five about which even less, or nothing at all, is known.

PLATE 1
Augusta Louise
Nothing is known about the ship which carried this figurehead beyond the fact that she was probably German and was believed to have been wrecked off the Orkneys. The figurehead was found at Kirkwall.

PLATE 2
Amphitrite
This very skilled model of a nude woman, unusually well carved, is probably from a nineteenth century barque; but there is nothing at all in the records to show either its origins or where it was found.

PLATE 3
Arabella
This was an iron barque of 688 tons, built at Sunderland in 1876 for Trinder Anderson and Company, as one of the "Ara" line (see the note on Bertha Marion). Cap'n Silver thought the figurehead probably represented a woman of the harem. There is no information about how he obtained it.

PLATE 4
Bertha Marion (later *Aralura,* later *Beda*)
This figurehead, a very handsome piece of work standing about ten feet high, is a good example of the problem of assigning names.

The ship, a composite barque of 540 tons, was built at Sunderland in 1864, and was owned by a Liverpool shipowner named Coghill. He named her after his daughter Bertha Marion Coghill. In 1879, after fifteen years as *Bertha Marion*, the ship was sold to Trinder Anderson and Company, and renamed *Aralura* in conformity with the company's practice of naming all their ships with names that began 'Ara'. In 1890, after eleven years as *Aralura*, she was sold again, this time to a Norwegian, A. P. Jonson of Landskrona. He renamed the ship *Beda*, after a Norwegian goddess. Silver was unable to trace what happened to the ship after that, but found the figurehead in the grounds of a house at Tiptree, Essex. For some reason he always referred to the figurehead as *Beda*, despite the fact that it was a portrait of Bertha Marion Coghill.

Plate 1: *Agusta Louise.*

Plate 2: *Amphitrite.*

Plate 3: *Arabella.*

Plate 4: *Bertha Marion (later Aralura, later Beda).*

Plate 5: *Cleopatra.*

Arabella **before restoration — see Plate 3.**

Because of its size and workmanship this carving occupied a place of honour in the display at Gravesend. There is also an account of Silver one day hearing someone talking in the room where the figurehead was kept, and on peering in saw the "stewardess", who was under five feet in height and whose duties included cleaning the displays, at the top of her ladder and scolding Bertha Marion as she washed her face.

PLATE 5
Cleopatra

There were at least three ships with this name built at about the same period. These were: an iron schooner of unknown weight built at Dumbarton in 1847; a brig of 187 tons built in about 1848, locality unknown; and a much larger ship of 1,233 tons built at Williamsburg, USA, in 1867.

There is nothing in any of the notes to suggest which ship the figurehead came from, and only the bare statement that the figurehead was found in Greenwich to give it any sort of provenance.

PLATE 6
Diana

This figurehead was first seen by Silver in the 'thirties in the possession of an 86-year old man named Wood. His father had helped build the ship, of 605 tons, at William Pitcher's Northfleet shipyard in 1799, and had also helped

34

to break it up when he was an old man. He had passed the figurehead to his son, who refused to part with it. After 1945 Silver tried to contact Mr. Wood again, to find that Mrs. Wood had died and that the old man, now very old indeed, had gone to live with relatives, and that in the course of doing so had sold the figurehead but could not remember to whom. A couple of years later still a general collector asked Silver to come and look at some figureheads to see if he wanted any of them and one of them was *Diana*. In all it took about twelve years from first sighting to acquisition.

The Wood family believed that the *Diana* had been to the Arctic to help in the search for Sir John Franklin, who was lost in about 1850 in attempting the Northwest passage. Two major expeditions were launched to look for Franklin, and any number of ships searched around if the occasion offered. His body was in the end found in 1859 on King William Island. The *Diana* was not named as being in any of the expeditions, but she might well of course have tried a private search. On the other hand the Greenwich Borough Chief Librarian wrote in 1947 to say that a ship named *Diana* had been on a voyage to Spitzbergen in 1873, and on another Arctic voyage in 1874; and this might have become confused with the earlier search for Franklin.

There are two problems about these accounts. First, there are the dates for the Wood father and son. If the son was 86 in the 'thirties he must have been born at the middle or just before the middle of the last century; and for his father to have helped build a ship in 1799 he must have been very young at the time, and also have gone on to have fathered a son in what was for those days very late in life. Still, it is possible.

Second, a ship of 605 tons, which is not very big, would have to be fairly lucky to survive for more than fifty years, especially if she was working the north Atlantic. Once again, however, it is possible.

PLATE 7
Disraeli (Lord Beaconsfield)

This was one of two figureheads (the other being the *Duchess*, now unidentifiable) found by Silver under the eaves of the sail loft of Beeching and Moses, ship builders at Ramsgate Harbour. He had first seen them when he was about seven or eight years old, and was much later told by a friend that they were being kept in a coal-shed on the Harbour Quay at Ramsgate. By then the local Council had taken over the Beeching and Moses yard, as it was part of the harbour, and agreed to sell the two figureheads. Silver never did find out anything useful about the *Duchess* beyond the fact that she was a barque broken up by Beeching and Moses. The *Disraeli* story was more complete, but on one point somewhat inconclusive.

There was a ship named *Disraeli* which was said to have been wrecked on the Goodwins in the early 1860's, and in pursuing this clue Silver was introduced through the correspondent of a local paper, *The Thanet Advertiser*, to Mr. Walter Moses, then eighty-four and the son of the founder of Beeching and Moses. The meeting was reported at length in *The Thanet Advertiser* on 8 March 1946. The wreck of the ship bearing the figurehead happened, Walter Moses claimed, at about the time he was

A view of the foc's'le at Gravesend.

born, which was 1862; but he remembered his father's account of it. The ship was trying to make Ramsgate Harbour in a strong gale, but on steering in was swung round, crashing her stern against the east pier head. She was then caught by the current, foundered on the east sands and became a total wreck. The derelict remains, including the figurehead, were bought by Thomas Moses, Walter Moses's father, and the figurehead was kept in the yard.

Everything ties in neatly, except that Walter Moses refused to budge from his conviction that the ship was called *The Lord Byron*. However, the figurehead certainly came from the Beeching and Moses yard, and whatever the defects of the carving, it is a lot more like Disraeli than Lord Byron. Unfortunately what records Beeching and Moses might have possessed have been lost, and there is now no way of settling the point. The balance of probabilities seem in favour of Disraeli.

PLATE 8
Eagle

Silver's conclusion was that this figurehead came from a full-rigged barque owned by Charles Hill and Sons of Bristol, and built by them in 1856. She eventually became a coal hulk.

The figurehead is a very fine piece of carving, but there is no record of how or when it was acquired. Among Silver's papers there is however a postcard showing a hulk at anchor, and on the back are pencil statements: "EAGLE Hulk at Gibraltar built USA 1859 Owned for some years by C. Hill and Sons of Bristol. Sold to J. Bland in 1885/86 and hulked at Gibraltar". There is therefore agreement that she was owned by Charles Hill and Sons, and that she became a hulk.

PLATE 9
Elizabeth Fry

This is thought to have been from a schooner built in 1864 which traded from Yarmouth, and was believed to have foundered in a gale. The figurehead was found in Norfolk. A Mr. R. Stuart Bruce wrote to the magazine *Sea Breezes* in 1934 saying that her nameboard had been washed ashore on the island of Yell in Shetland in February 1871. There were at least two other ships, apart from the 1864

Eagle as a hulk at Gibraltar — see Plate 8.

35

Plate 6: *Diana.*

Plate 7: *Disraeli (Lord Beaconsfield).*

Plate 8: *Eagle.*

Plate 9: *Elizabeth Fry.*

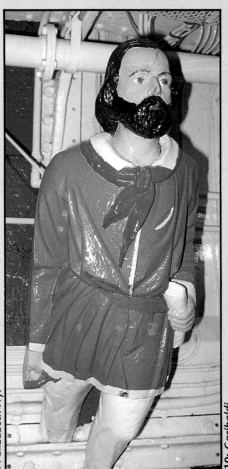

Plate 10: *Garibaldi.*

Plate 11: *Gladstone.*

Plate 12: *Golden Cherubs.*

Plate 13: *General Gordon.*

one, named *Elizabeth Fry*. One, of 1,094 tons, was built in 1861 at St. Johns, New Brunswick for S. Gardnies of Liverpool. She was taken out of Lloyds Register in 1874. The other was owned in North Shields in 1880 by F. Dale and Company, and was out of Register in 1885. In a brochure issued in 1946 for a special exhibition at The Look-Out Silver gave a date of 1861 for the figurehead, which suggests that at that time he thought she was from the St. Johns ship; but all the later notes refer to the 1864 schooner.

The figurehead is shown with an umbrella in one hand and what Silver in his notes always described as a prayer book in the other; but if it really is Elizabeth Fry a prayer book is most unlikely. Elizabeth Fry (1780-1845) was a life-long Quaker from a well known Quaker family who married another eminent Quaker. She was a philanthropist and prison reformer and she might well have carried a copy of the New Testament, but a prayer book, peculiar to the Church of England, is highly improbable. Margery Fry, a distant relative, wrote to Silver in 1944 saying that the figurehead's costume did not look like the Quaker costume of cap, bonnet and fichu which she wore throughout her adult life; but the carver might of course have taken liberties with his representation of her dress and simply have shown what he thought she ought to have been wearing. It does look like popular representations of her, and the recovery of the nameboard at about the right date makes it a bit more probable.

PLATE 10
Garibaldi

Guiseppe Garibaldi (1807-1882) was an Italian patriot and soldier of fortune who played a major part in the creation of the modern Italian state. He received a wildly enthusiastic reception when he visited England in 1864. A woman's loose blouse in imitation of those worn by his soldiers became very popular at the time and was called a Garibaldi. It was originally red, because that was the colour used by Garibaldi, but the name was later used for almost any loose blouse or jacket. There was also a woman's hat named after him and, somewhat more improbably, a biscuit with a layer of currants. He served for about ten years in South America, and there is a Californian red perch which is also called a Garibaldi.

Silver's records say nothing about either the figurehead or the ship from which it came, beyond the short statement that the ship was wrecked on the Orkney Islands.

PLATE 11
Gladstone

William Ewart Gladstone (1809-1898) was, with Disraeli, a dominant figure in British politics in the second half of the nineteenth century. The figurehead is a passable representation of him in his middle years, but one of Silver's notes suggests it might be John Bright. Bright, a Quaker and a radical, was another outstanding political figure and almost the same age as Gladstone, being born two years later but dying nine years earlier.

There is no information in the Silver records about either the ship or the figurehead.

38

PLATE 12
Golden Cherubs

This was spotted by Silver while on holiday at Bude in Cornwall in 1936. There were two figureheads at a wood carving and antiques shop, one of them more or less complete, but the other in pieces. When he examined them later at home he discovered that the one in a better state of repair was fairly ordinary, but that the broken one was clearly old and a rare piece of carving. He brought in an antique restorer, a Mr. W. Arbin, to help repair it and started on the task of tracing its history. The wood is west Indian pine, which began to be used towards the end of the reign of Charles I and became very popular at the end of the seventeenth century for panelled rooms and mantlepieces. When the paint and dirt had been removed they discovered that the fiddle (the banner-like plaque) which holds the cherubs in position was carved with a galleon, and had underneath a swag of fruit and leaves. The galleon could plausibly be regarded as a representation of the original ship and the cherubs, and the swag of fruit and leaves, were characteristically in the style of Grinling Gibbons. Moreover, there are said to be records of Gibbons working at Deptford on ship's carvings. The not unreasonable conclusion was that the figurehead was indeed carved by Grinling Gibbons; and if so, the only one known to be in existence, as well as being the oldest merchant marine figurehead known.

The story of the ship from which the figurehead probably came is equally interesting. It belonged to a Cornish smuggler and wrecker named Thomas Jacobs, who had her built about 1660. He was the leading figure in a gang consisting of Simon Symonds, master of the port of Bude and allegedly not only one-eyed but one-legged as well; and three further men named Dee, Saunders, and Copinger. They used the ship for smuggling and whatever else came their way. An exciseman named John Silver was sent down to investigate the smuggling and was scheduled to arrive on 27 March 1673. For some reason he did not arrive until 1 April and was met by Simon Symonds and the rest of the company. Symonds chose to make the delay in arriving an excuse to pick a quarrel. Silver (that is Sydney Cumbers) in his notes gives a spirited account of what followed, based on local stories and legends. The argument ended with Symonds decapitating John Silver with his cutlas. His head was

Hiawatha (later *Fiskjo*) being towed into Dover — see Plate 14.

concealed in a wall of the building, and his body lashed to his horse, which was driven over the sandhills towards the sea and seen no more. The head is said to have been found relatively recently during excavations of an old cottage, and there is indeed somewhere a photograph (which Silver saw) of a skull embedded in a wall. Thomas Jacobs and his gang continued their smuggling until they and the ship were lost in a storm off Tintagel in 1703.

In his notes Silver wondered whether R. L. Stevenson had come across the story and used it as the starting point for the characters in Treasure Island. The picture shows Silver with the figurehead and a contemporary painting of Jacobs which he acquired.

PLATE 13
General Gordon

General Charles George Gordon (1833–1885) was a very popular figure in mid-Victorian England. He served in the Crimea as a young man; then in China during the Taiping Rebellion (1864), where he earned the nickname Chinese Gordon; and then in the Sudan, where he was killed at Khartoum shortly before it was relieved in 1885. There is little doubt the figurehead corresponds with popular representations of Gordon, but there is nothing in the Silver records beyond the brief note that it was from a brigantine.

PLATE 14
Hiawatha (later Fiskjo)

The *Hiawatha* was a steel ship of 1,498 tons, and was built in 1891 at Dumbarton by Archibald MacMillan and Son for H. Bjorn Jnr of Kragero, Norway. He kept her until 1917, and then sold her to a Mr. Hansen of Kristiansand, who renamed her *Fiskjo*. In 1924 she was sold to the Dover Shipbreaking Company. Silver was tipped off by a dealer in Cardiff, and found the figurehead in a garden at Kearney, near Dover.

There were three other ships with the same name. The first was a brig of 280 tons built at Prince Edward Island in 1871; the second a wooden barque of 934 tons built in Nova Scotia in 1876; and the third another barque of 280 tons built in New Brunswick in 1878. There seems no doubt however about the provenance of this figurehead.

The figurehead itself is a splendid representation of a North American Indian standing nearly ten feet high and estimated to weigh about half a ton. The black and white photograph is from a post card produced by Amos and Amos of Dover.

PLATE 15
Hunter

This was a wooden barque of 500 tons, built in 1854. For a relatively small ship it is a large figurehead, over nine feet high. There is no information about what happened to the ship, or where the figurehead was found.

PLATE 16
Sophie Kirk (later Regia, later Anirac)

This was a steel barque of 959 tons built in 1893 by Workman Clark at Belfast for A. Craig of Belfast, and was a sister ship to the *Jeannie Woodside*. She was sold in 1910 to Norway and renamed *Regia*; and she was sold

Sketch of *Sir Lancelot* bows by George F. Campbell, 1974 — see Plate 17.

again in 1912 to Italy and renamed *Anirac*. She is believed to have been wrecked in February 1913.

There is no record about how or where the figurehead was acquired.

PLATE 17
Sir Lancelot

Although the name was entered in Silver's notes as conjectural, it seems fairly safe. The book *China Tea Clippers* by George F. Campbell (1974) gives some information about the ship, and in a drawing he made of the bow and figurehead of it he clearly used this figurehead from the Silver Collection, which he knew well.

Sir Lancelot was a British clipper, built in 1865 by R. Steele for John MacCunn of Hull. At 886 tons she was slightly smaller than the *Cutty Sark*. Campbell has an account of her having a very bad time in 1866 on her second voyage, when she ran into a severe storm in the Channel, outward bound. She lost her bowsprit, the whole of the mainmast and of the foremast, and the mizzenmast top. By what Campbell calls Herculean efforts they managed to erect a jury mast on the stump of the foremast, and in what was described as the most vicious winter in fifty years manoeuvred her unaided into Falmouth. Six weeks later she was on her way again, fully repaired, heading for China.

She remained on Lloyds Register for the next thirty years, being sold to Visram Ebrahim and Company in 1888, and then to Haji Abdulla. In the Register for 1896/97 however she was entered as missing since May 1895.

There are no notes in Silver's records about where or when the figurehead was found.

PLATE 18
Lincoln

This was a wooden barque of 688 tons built in 1865 by J. Strandberg of Hernosand for A. Matterquist, also of Hernosand. It is believed to have been wrecked off Black Gang Chine, in the south of the Isle of Wight.

HIAWATHA
From a steel ship of 1049 tons built by Archibald McMillan & Son of Dumbarton in 1894, for a Norwegian owner. She was sold to another Norwegian in 1917 and renamed Fiskjo. She was...

Plate 14: *Hiawatha (later Fiskjo).*

HUNTER
From a wooden barque of four guns, built in 1854. Her length was 174 feet and her beam 28...

Plate 15: *Hunter.*

Plate 16: *Sophie Kirk (later Regia, later Anirac).*

Plate 17: *Sir Lancelot.*

Plate 18: *Lincoln.*

40

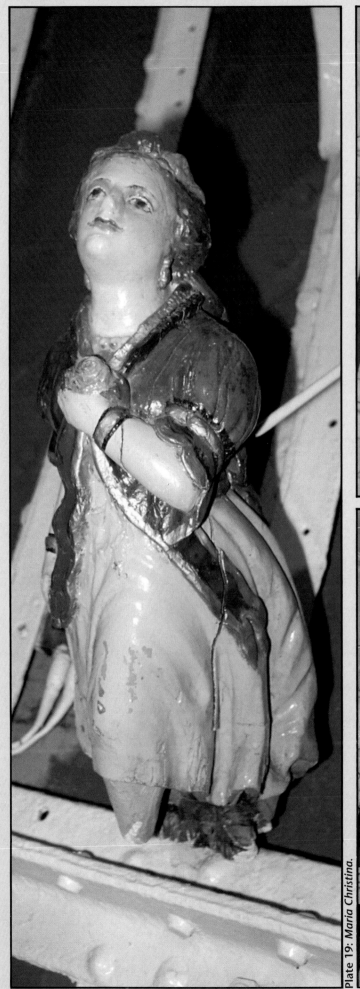

Plate 19: *Maria Christina.*

Plate 20: *Marianne.*

Plate 21: *Maude.*

41

The notes say that the figurehead was found at Quayle in the Isle of Wight, and a further note says that according to the magazine *Neptunia* the figurehead is carved in teak, including the beard.

PLATE 19
Maria Christina

This was a wooden schooner of 106 tons, built in 1864 by J. P. Wickman of Skelinge, Sweden. She was wrecked on Doom Bar off Padstow in 1930.

There is no record of how or where the figurehead was acquired.

PLATE 20
Marianne

There is little doubt that this figurehead represents the French Marianne, but nothing is known about the ship from which it came. It may perhaps have been a French Grand Banker, probably either a tunney fishing boat from Concarneau, or a cod fisher from St. Malo. Professor P. Bohé in the Paris journal *Neptunia* agreed in 1951 that it was Marianne, but thought it more likely the ship was a cod fisher from either St. Malo or the Rance.

PLATE 21
Maude

This was a barque of 1,108 tons, built in 1878 by R. and J. Evans of Liverpool for themselves. One note claims she was sold in 1897 to Brazilian owners and wrecked in 1899 at an unknown place; but all the other notes say she was a general trader which later became an isolation hospital ship at Plymouth. One of them also adds that she was affectionately known to the medical officers at the port as Maudie.

There is no record about how or where the figurehead was acquired.

PLATE 22
Nannie (the *Cutty Sark*)

Nannie is the name of the figurehead of the *Cutty Sark*, and is taken from Robert Burns' poem "Tam O'Shanter". The story is that Tam, after an evening of drinking with friends, was riding home and on the way saw that the churchyard of Kirk Alloway was occupied by a collection of warlocks and witches dancing to music provided by the Devil. Most of them were ugly but one of them was beautiful, and wearing nothing but an indecently short petticoat or shift, which in the vernacular was called a cutty sark. Tam, without thinking, cried out in admiration as she danced, and the whole pack turned on him. He fled as fast as his horse Maggie could run and only just made it. As Maggie galloped over the bridge across the Doon (and witches cannot cross running water) Nannie came close enough to catch the horse's tail and tear it off. Hence, the figurehead is always shown holding a horse's tail in her left hand.

John Willis, who commissioned and owned the *Cutty Sark* until he sold her to the Portuguese in 1895, was a Scot, but there is nothing in the records to suggest why he named his latest and favourite ship after the then slightly indelicate cutty sark. However, he not only did, but had a metal emblem made in the form of a cutty sark which was worn at the mainmast when the ship was in port.

The Look-Out — the foc's'le looking through the quarter deck. The arch in the doorway is the centre of the port-side paddle box of the small excursion steamer *Southend Belle*.

The original figurehead was carved by F. Hellyer of Blackwall, a member of a very well known carving family, but the head and left arm were lost in rough weather sometime between 1885 and 1895. The figurehead now mounted in the usual place on the prow of the ship as she rides in her dry dock at Greenwich is a replacement made in 1956 by Arthur Levinson from Columbian pine presented by the Canadian Lumbermen's Association to the Cutty Sark Society. Some years later the dismembered original was found on board and in 1969/70 was repaired by Jack Whitehead. This is the one now mounted on board near the entrance on the 'tween deck, and her left hand holds a genuine horse's tail. In the days when she was still sailing, the tail used to be made out of old rope, teased out by the apprentices on board.

The *Cutty Sark*, of 963 tons, was built on the Clyde and sailed on her maiden voyage in February 1870. She was sold to the Portuguese in 1895, and in 1923 bought from them by Captain Wilfred Dowman. He died in 1936 and his widow presented her to the Thames Nautical Training College. In 1953 she was formally presented to the Cutty Sark Society, and after being settled in a specially built dry dock, repaired and re-rigged, she was opened to the public by the Queen on 25 June 1957.

PLATE 23
Naval Officer (USA)

Nothing at all is known about either the ship or the figurehead. The style of costume is said to date it as an American officer of about the 1860's.

PLATE 24
Navarino

This was a trading brig which went ashore at Pegwell Bay in 1863 while trying to enter Ramsgate Harbour. Silver spotted it in the Queen's Head Hotel in Ramsgate, mounted on the wall above the bar. The landlord said his grandfather had collected it from the wreck, but refused to sell it.

At the outset of the 1939–45 War the hotel was closed, the figurehead with the other fittings put in store, and the landlord and his family moved to a village near Tunbridge Wells. After the end of the war he wrote to Silver saying that if he still wanted *Navarino* he could have it. The deal was agreed, and the figurehead was brought to Gravesend by the tug *Arcadia*.

PLATE 25
Florence Nightingale

This is believed to have been a schooner which traded in the Mediterranean. The figurehead is thought to have come from Malta at the beginning of the century, and probably represents Florence Nightingale as a young woman. If the attribution is correct, it would probably be post-Crimean War (i.e. after 1856) because she was not a very well known public figure prior to her intervention in the Crimea.

There is nothing in the notes about either the ship or the figurehead.

PLATE 26
Old Goody

This was a wooden schooner of 174 tons, built by Paine at Sandwich for E. Rigden of Whitstable. She is said to have traded regularly into Ramsgate with coal. There is no reference to her being wrecked or lost, and she was presumably broken up in old age.

The figurehead was rescued, and for some time mounted over the door to a butcher's shop in Faversham before making her way to the Silver Collection.

PLATE 27
Omar Pasha

This was a brig of 225 tons, built in 1854 in Nova Scotia for one Blythe. The figurehead was brought from Malta in the early 1880's by Mr. Wyndham, the Superintendent of the Mercantile Dockyard. It was eventually found at Croydon. The head is unusual, although not unique (because Silver had at least one other similar one), in having glass eyes.

Omar Pasha (1806-1871) was a highly colourful character who became prominent before and during the Crimean War. He was born Michael Latas in Croatia, served in the Austrian Army, and then deserted, became a Mohammedan and rose rapidly to become a general in the army of the Ottoman Empire. He fought on the British/French side in the Crimean War, and in his career defeated Russian armies at least three times.

PLATE 28
Ophir

The *Ophir* was a wooden barque of 449 tons built at Arendal in Norway by Tellef Larsen in 1874 for H. H. Pettersen of Arendal. She was wrecked off Worthing on 6 December 1896. The figurehead is a representation of King Solomon, with a gold crown and purple robe.

The figurehead was found in the front garden of a house at Notting Hill Gate, the owner having bought it from the widow of a ship's captain who apparently either knew the ship or served on her.

PLATE 29
Pitt

The probability is that this figurehead represents William Pitt the Younger. It was found at Croydon, and was said to have come from Malta. A part from these two facts there is nothing in any of the notes about either the figurehead or the ship from which it came.

PLATE 30
Lalla Rookh

Lalla Rookh was the heroine of a poem by Thomas Moore, first published in 1817 and enormously popular, with many editions and translations into Danish, Dutch, French, German, Italian, Icelandic and Polish. Silver traced two ships with this name, and there is a manuscript note in the records of a third possibility about which nothing is known beyond the suggestion that she was an iron barque of 794 tons built in 1879. Of the other two, the first was built in 1856 and the second in 1876, but Silver had seen a photograph of the 1876 ship's figurehead and it bore no resemblance to the one in his

Plate 22: *Nannie (the Cutty Sark).*

Plate 23: *Naval Officer (USA).*

Plate 24: *Navarino.*

Plate 25: *Florence Nightingale.*

44

Plate 26: Old Goody.

Plate 27: Omar Pasha.

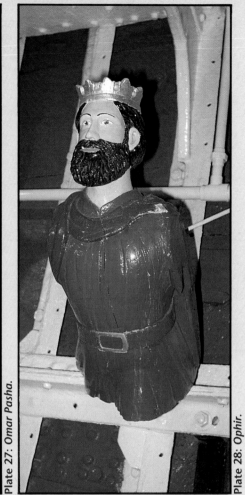

Plate 28: Ophir.

Plate 29: Pitt.

Plate 30: Lalla Rookh.

collection. The figurehead was found in Jersey immediately before the 1939-45 War, and was brought out just in time to escape the German occupation in 1940. It is reasonably certain she is from the the 1856 ship.

The ship was wrecked on Prawle Point, Devon, in 1873 on her way home from Shanghai. She was an iron ship of 869 tons, owned by Prowse and Company of Liverpool, and for her last voyage was commanded by Captain George Fullarton. She left Shanghai on 22 October 1872 and by March 1873 was near home. It was a very foggy night and the ship, possibly through a faulty compass reading, came too close to land and struck a rock at Gammon Head, about half a mile west of Prawle Point. Anchors were let go, but the ship drifted on to the sand in a little cove between cliffs. They were so close to the rocks that four of the crew were able to jump on to them and save themselves. The mate was unfortunately drowned in an attempt to launch a boat. The coastguards, alerted by one of the men who had jumped ashore, brought out their rocket apparatus and in the end fifteen men, including Captain Fullarton, were saved. The only losses were the mate and a young stowaway who had been very ill during the voyage and was thought to have died before the ship struck. The *Kingsbridge Gazette* published on 22 March 1873 a letter from the carpenter, Joseph John Blundell, thanking the coastguards on behalf of the crew, commending their rocket apparatus, and expressing the crew's gratitude to the people of Prawle who had looked after them.

Mrs. Rosalind Douglas, who was Captain Fullarton's niece, later recorded that her uncle had kept on board a painting of her which was lost in the wreck. About ten or twelve years later while having his hair cut in Liverpool Fullarton found that the young barber came from Salcombe, near Prawle, and asked casually if he remembered the loss of the *Lalla Rookh*. He said: "Oh, yes. I picked up the top of the captain's chronometer and a picture of a curly-haired little girl." Fullarton explained who he was, and that the little girl was his niece; and the barber presented the painting to him. He later passed it to Mrs. Douglas.

PLATE 31
Lady of the Rose

This figurehead, which stands about ten feet high. was described by Silver as: "undoubtedly . . . the finest carved figurehead in the whole collection", but despite all his efforts over several years he was unable to find out the name of the ship from which it came .

The figurehead was originally found in a very dilapidated condition in English's Wood Yard at Wisbech, Cambridge, by a second-hand dealer, from whom it was bought by a Mr. Ihlee of Peterborough in about 1923. The local rumour was that the ship had been wrecked off the Norfolk coast. Mr. Ihlee handed the carving over to Mr. C. J. Hayward to restore, and Silver was in correspondence with him when Hayward was getting on for ninety. Hayward said he had taken a long time restoring the figurehead, working in his spare time, and that once restored it was put at the top of the staircase in Paston Hall, Peterborough. This accounted for the relatively good state of preservation it was in when Silver acquired her.

Lalla Rookh in port — see Plate 30.

Silver later came across a portrait of Mrs. Felicia Hemans, the author among many other things of *Casabianca*, and thought she looked very like the carving. Mrs. Hemans lived at one time at Wavertree, Liverpool, so there was a plausible shipping connection, and she was at the height of her considerable fame in the 1830's. He also wondered whether, alternatively, the ship was one of the French nitrite ships, which were noted for their female figureheads; and one of his notes suggests she might have been Hélène. Nevertheless, in all the notes and correspondence no one was able to provide any definite information about the ship.

PLATE 32
Spring (later *Gravesend*)

This was a wooden topsail schooner of 136 tons, built by W. Dale of Kingsbridge, Devon, in 1867 for Yabley and Company of Salcombe. It was built for the West Indian fruit trade, and known accordingly as a Salcombe fruiterer. She was a fast and tough little ship, and was one of the last schooners to be tiller steered. She was sold in 1888 to Rillston and Company of Fowey, and then sold again in 1892 to W. Bromley of London and renamed *Gravesend*. For some years she carried coals from the north to Gravesend, and ended up as a powder hulk in Gravesend Reach in the Thames estuary. A rather poor photograph, undated, has survived showing her under sail.

The figurehead was found supporting the corner of a chicken house in a back garden, but none of the notes say where this was.

PLATE 33
Sovereign

This figurehead is from a brig of the same name, but nothing else is recorded about it. It represents a Saxon king, and the right arm is detachable so that it could be unshipped in heavy weather.